C000318680

Exley Publications Ltd,
16 Chalk Hill, Watford, Herts WD19 4BG, United Kingdom.
Exley Publications LLC, 185 Main Street, Spencer, MA 01562, USA.
www.helenexleygiftbooks.com

Published simultaneously in the USA by Exley Publications LLC and
in Great Britain by Exley Publications Ltd, 2003

12 11 10 9 8 7 6 5 4 3 2 1

ISBN 1-86187-533-9

Edited by Helen Exley.
Pictures researched by Image Select International.
Designed by 451°. Printed in China.

Exley Publications is very grateful to the following individuals and
organizations for permission to reproduce their pictures: Atkinson Art
Gallery, Southport: page 30; Bonhams, London: page 46; Bridgeman Art
Library: pages 6, 7, 14, 22, 57; City of Bristol Museum: pages 52, 53;
Christies Colour Library: page 11; Coram Foundation, London: page 55;
John Davies Fine Paintings: page 9; © Ditz "Mother and Child": page 34;
Fine Art Photographic: pages 25, 28; Mary Evans Picture Library: pages
19, 37; Musee D'Orsay, Paris: pages 12, 13, 44, 45; National Museum,
Stockholm: cover and page 16: Carl Larsson, "A Studio Idyll: The Artist's
Wife and their Daughter Suzanne"; Oldham Art Gallery: pages 27, 50;
Phillips Auctioneers: pages 48, 49; Scala: pages 5, 39, 42, 59; Turko Art
Museum: page 40; Waterhouse & Dodd, London: page 33; Whitford &
Hughes, London: page 61; Christopher Wood Art Gallery: pages 20, 21.

Words of love about
Mothers

A HELEN EXLEY GIFTBOOK

SHE IS THEIR EARTH… SHE IS THEIR FOOD AND THEIR BED AND THE EXTRA BLANKET WHEN IT GROWS COLD IN THE NIGHT; SHE IS THEIR WARMTH AND THEIR HEALTH AND THEIR SHELTER…

katharine butler hathaway

WHEN YOU ARE A MOTHER, YOU ARE NEVER
REALLY ALONE IN YOUR THOUGHTS. YOU ARE
CONNECTED TO YOUR CHILD AND TO ALL THOSE
WHO TOUCH YOUR LIVES.

sophia loren, b.1934

IT'S THE THREE PAIRS OF EYES
THAT MOTHERS HAVE TO HAVE...
ONE PAIR THAT SEE THROUGH CLOSED DOORS.
ANOTHER IN THE BACK OF HER HEAD... AND,
OF COURSE, THE ONES IN FRONT THAT CAN LOOK
AT A CHILD WHEN HE GOOFS UP AND REFLECT
"I UNDERSTAND AND I LOVE YOU" WITHOUT SO
MUCH AS UTTERING A WORD.

erma bombeck, b.1927

that powerful connection

A MOTHER ALWAYS HAS TO THINK TWICE,

ONCE FOR HERSELF AND ONCE FOR HER CHILD.

*sophia loren, b.*1934

A MOTHER'S CHILDREN ARE LIKE IDEAS;
NONE ARE AS WONDERFUL AS HER OWN.

chinese fortune

always proud

MY POINT IS THAT NO MATTER WHAT THE ORDINARY
PERSON SAYS... NO MATTER WHO IT IS THAT SPEAKS,
OR WHAT SUPERLATIVES ARE EMPLOYED, NO BABY IS
ADMIRED SUFFICIENTLY TO PLEASE THE MOTHER.

e. v. lucas

A MOTHER DOESN'T GIVE A DAMN ABOUT YOUR
LOOKS. *SHE* THINKS YOU ARE BEAUTIFUL, ANYWAY.

marion c. garretty, b.1917

I SHALL NEVER FORGET MY MOTHER,
FOR IT WAS SHE WHO PLANTED AND NURTURED
THE FIRST SEEDS OF GOOD WITHIN ME. SHE OPENED
MY HEART TO THE IMPRESSIONS OF NATURE;
SHE AWAKENED MY UNDERSTANDING AND EXTENDED
MY HORIZON, AND HER PERCEPTS EXERTED AN EVERLASTING
INFLUENCE UPON THE COURSE OF MY LIFE.

immanuel kant (1724 - 1804)

THOU ARE THY MOTHER'S GLASS, AND SHE IN THEE
CALLS BACK THE LOVELY APRIL OF HER PRIME.

william shakespeare (1564 - 1616)

THEY ALWAYS LOOKED BACK BEFORE TURNING
THE CORNER, FOR THEIR MOTHER WAS ALWAYS AT THE
WINDOW TO NOD AND SMILE, AND WAVE HER HAND
AT THEM. SOMEHOW IT SEEMED AS IF THEY COULDN'T HAVE
GOT THROUGH THE DAY WITHOUT THAT, FOR WHATEVER
THEIR MOOD MIGHT BE, THE LAST GLIMPSE OF THAT
MOTHERLY FACE WAS SURE TO AFFECT
THEM LIKE SUNSHINE.

louisa may alcott (1832 - 1888)

like sunshine

SHE BRINGS THE SUNSHINE INTO THE HOUSE; IT IS
NOW A PLEASURE TO BE THERE.

cecil beaton (1904 - 1980)

SUDDENLY SHE WAS HERE. AND I WAS
NO LONGER PREGNANT; I WAS A MOTHER.
I NEVER BELIEVED IN MIRACLES BEFORE.

ellen greene

thoughts of
a new mother

I LOVE BEING A MOTHER. I AM MORE AWARE.
I FEEL THINGS ON A DEEPER LEVEL. I SEEM TO
HAVE MORE OF EVERYTHING NOW: MORE LOVE,
MORE MAGIC, MORE ENERGY.

shelley long

THOU, STRAGGLER INTO LOVING ARMS,
YOUNG CLIMBER UP OF KNEES,
WHEN I FORGET THY THOUSAND WAYS,
THEN LIFE AND ALL SHALL CEASE.

mary lamb (1764 - 1847)

protector

EVERYBODY KNOWS THAT A GOOD MOTHER GIVES HER
CHILDREN A FEELING OF TRUST AND STABILITY.
SOMEHOW EVEN HER CLOTHES FEEL DIFFERENT TO
HER CHILDREN'S HANDS FROM ANYBODY ELSE'S
CLOTHES. ONLY TO TOUCH HER SKIRT OR HER SLEEVE
MAKES A TROUBLED CHILD FEEL BETTER.

katharine butler hathaway

THE CHILD, IN THE DECISIVE FIRST YEARS
OF HIS LIFE, HAS THE EXPERIENCE OF HIS MOTHER,
AS AN ALL-ENVELOPING, PROTECTIVE,
NOURISHING POWER. MOTHER IS FOOD; SHE IS LOVE;
SHE IS WARMTH; SHE IS EARTH. TO BE LOVED BY HER
MEANS TO BE ALIVE, TO BE ROOTED,
TO BE AT HOME.

erich fromm (1900 - 1980)

A MOTHER IS A PERSON WHO IF SHE IS NOT
THERE WHEN YOU GET HOME FROM SCHOOL
YOU WOULDN'T KNOW HOW TO GET YOUR
DINNER, AND YOU WOULDN'T FEEL LIKE
EATING IT ANYWAY.

anonymous

Now, as always, the most automated
appliance in a household is the mother.

*beverley jones, b.*1927

Any mother could perform the jobs of several
air-traffic controllers with ease.

lisa alther

Mother's Wrinkled Hands

Such beautiful, beautiful hands!
Though heart was weary and sad
Those patient hands kept toiling on
That her children might be glad.
I almost weep when looking back
To childhood's distant day!
I think how these hands rested not
When mine were at their play.

unknown

WE BEAR THE WORLD, AND WE MAKE IT.... THERE
WAS NEVER A GREAT MAN WHO HAD NOT A GREAT
MOTHER — IT IS HARDLY AN EXAGGERATION.

olive schreiner (1855 - 1920)

EVERY BREATH SHE EVER BREATHED, EVERY EFFORT
SHE EVER MADE, EVERY PRAYER SHE EVER PRAYED
WAS FOR HER SON.... THE GREATEST BREAK THAT
FRANCIS ALBERT SINATRA EVER ENJOYED IN HIS
ENTIRE LIFE, IN HIS ENTIRE CAREER, WAS TO HAVE
DOLLY AS A MOTHER.

reverend robert perella

MY MOTHER WAS THE MOST BEAUTIFUL WOMAN....
ALL I AM I OWE TO MY MOTHER.... I ATTRIBUTE ALL MY
SUCCESS IN LIFE TO THE MORAL, INTELLECTUAL AND
PHYSICAL EDUCATION I RECEIVED FROM HER.

george washington (1732 - 1799)

A MOTHER UNDERSTANDS WHAT A CHILD DOES NOT SAY.

jewish proverb

MOTHER, I LOVE YOU SO.
SAID THE CHILD, I LOVE YOU MORE THAN I KNOW.
SHE LAID HER HEAD ON HER MOTHER'S ARM,
AND THE LOVE BETWEEN THEM KEPT THEM WARM.

stevie smith (1902 - 1971)

TO MY MOTHER I TELL THE TRUTH. I HAVE NO
THOUGHT, NO FEELING THAT I CANNOT SHARE WITH
MY MOTHER, AND SHE IS LIKE A SECOND
CONSCIENCE TO ME, HER EYES LIKE A MIRROR
REFLECTING MY OWN IMAGE.

william gerhardi (1895 - 1977)

I WOULD DESIRE FOR A FRIEND THE SON WHO NEVER
RESISTED THE TEARS OF HIS MOTHER.

lacretelle

A MAN LOVES HIS SWEETHEART THE MOST, HIS WIFE
THE BEST, BUT HIS MOTHER THE LONGEST.

irish proverb

EVERY MAN, FOR THE SAKE OF THE GREAT BLESSED
MOTHER IN HEAVEN, AND FOR THE LOVE OF
HIS OWN LITTLE MOTHER ON EARTH, SHOULD
HANDLE ALL WOMANKIND GENTLY, AND HOLD
THEM IN ALL HONOUR.

alfred, lord tennyson (1809 - 1892)

THAT IF A MAN LOVES HIS MOTHER HE WILL ALWAYS

LOVE HIS WIFE.

george jean nathan

THAT DEAR OCTOPUS FROM WHOSE TENTACLES WE
NEVER QUITE ESCAPE, NOR IN OUR INNERMOST
HEARTS NEVER QUITE WISH TO.

dodie smith (1896 - 1990)

PART OF US RESENTS FOREVER THE FACT THAT WE
AND OUR MOTHERS WERE CLOSER THAN WE CAN EVER
BE TO ANY OTHER CREATURE. THEY GAVE US
FREEDOM — BUT WE SENSE THE HIDDEN BOND,
AND KNOW IT'S UNBREAKABLE.

*pam brown, b.*1928

SOME ARE KISSING MOTHERS AND SOME
ARE SCOLDING MOTHERS, BUT IT IS LOVE
JUST THE SAME, AND MOST MOTHERS KISS
AND SCOLD TOGETHER.

pearl s. buck (1892 - 1973)

true riches

A RICH CHILD OFTEN SITS IN A POOR
MOTHER'S LAP.

danish proverb

Haec Ornamenta Sunt Mea

CORNELIA, THE MOTHER OF THE GRACCHI,
ONCE ENTERTAINED A WOMAN FROM CAMPANIA
AT HER HOUSE. SINCE THE WOMAN MADE A
GREAT SHOW OF HER JEWELS, WHICH WERE
AMONG THE MOST BEAUTIFUL OF THE TIME,
CORNELIA DETAINED HER IN CONVERSATION
UNTIL HER CHILDREN CAME HOME FROM
SCHOOL. THEN, POINTING TO HER CHILDREN,
SHE SAID, "THESE ARE MY JEWELS."

valerius maximus 1st century

WHAT IS TRULY INDISPENSIBLE FOR THE CONDUCT
OF LIFE HAS BEEN TAUGHT US BY WOMEN — THE
SMALL RULES OF COURTESY, THE ACTIONS THAT WIN
US THE WARMTH OR DEFERENCE OF OTHERS; THE
WORDS THAT ASSURE US A WELCOME; THE ATTITUDES
THAT MUST BE VARIED TO MESH WITH CHARACTER OR
SITUATION; ALL SOCIAL STRATEGY.

remy de gourmont (1858 - 1915)

THEY SAY THAT MAN IS MIGHTY,
HE GOVERNS LAND AND SEA,
HE WIELDS A MIGHTY SCEPTRE,
O'ER LESSER POWERS THAT BE,
BUT A MIGHTIER POWER AND STRONGER,
MAN FROM HIS THRONE HAS HURLED,
FOR THE HAND THAT ROCKS THE CRADLE,
IS THE HAND THAT RULES THE WORLD.

william ross wallace

WOMAN IS THE SALVATION OR DESTRUCTION
OF THE FAMILY.
SHE CARRIES ITS DESTINIES IN THE FOLDS OF
HER MANTLE.

henri-frederic amiel (1821 - 1881)

IN THE SHELTERED SIMPLICITY OF THE FIRST DAYS
AFTER A BABY IS BORN, ONE SEES AGAIN THE
MAGICAL CLOSED CIRCLE, THE MIRACULOUS SENSE OF
TWO PEOPLE EXISTING ONLY FOR EACH OTHER.

anne morrow lindbergh (1906 - 2001)

THE VERY WORD "MOTHERHOOD" HAS AN
EMOTIONAL DEPTH AND SIGNIFICANCE FEW TERMS
HAVE. IT BESPEAKS NOURISHMENT AND SAFETY AND
SHELTERING ARMS. IT EMBRACES NOT ONLY THE
HUMAN STATE BUT THE ANIMAL KINGDOM — THE
TIGER FIERCELY PROTECTIVE OF HER CUBS, THE HEN
CLUCKING OVER HER BROOD AND SPREADING HER
WINGS TO SHIELD THEM FROM THE STORM.
IT SPEAKS OF THE VERY BEGINNINGS OF LIFE IN
EGG OR WOMB AND OF NURTURE IN THE MOST
CRITICAL STAGES THEREAFTER.

marjorie holmes

IN MY INTEREST SHE LEFT NO WIRE UNPULLED,
NO STONE UNTURNED, NO CUTLET UNCOOKED.

winston churchill (1875 - 1965),
on his mother, Jennie Jerome Churchill

FIFTY-FOUR YEARS OF LOVE AND TENDERNESS AND
CROSSNESS AND DEVOTION AND UNSWERVING
LOYALTY. WITHOUT HER I COULD HAVE ACHIEVED
A QUARTER OF WHAT I HAVE ACHIEVED, NOT ONLY IN
TERMS OF SUCCESS AND CAREER, BUT IN TERMS OF
PERSONAL HAPPINESS.... SHE HAS NEVER STOOD
BETWEEN ME AND MY LIFE, NEVER TRIED TO HOLD
ME TOO TIGHTLY, ALWAYS LET ME GO FREE....

noel coward (1899 - 1973)

MY MOTHER'S LOVE FOR ME WAS SO GREAT
THAT I HAVE WORKED HARD TO JUSTIFY IT.

marc chagall (1889 - 1985),
just before his ninetieth birthday

My mother was the making of me. She was so true and so sure of me, I felt that I had someone to live for — someone I must not disappoint. The memory of my mother will always be a blessing to me.

thomas a. edison (1847 - 1931)

1 unconditional *love*

IN THE EYES OF THE MOTHER EVERY
BEETLE IS A GAZELLE.

moroccan proverb

WHO IS IT THAT LOVES ME AND WILL LOVE ME FOR
EVER WITH AN AFFECTION WHICH NO CHANCE,
NO MISERY, NO CRIME OF MINE CAN DO AWAY?
IT IS YOU, MY MOTHER.

thomas carlyle, (1795 - 1881)
from a letter to his mother

WHICH ONE?

dwight d. eisenhower's mother,
on being asked if she was proud of her son

there are no poor mothers

I GOT MORE CHILDREN THAN I CAN RIGHTLY TAKE
CARE OF, BUT I AIN'T GOT MORE THAN I CAN LOVE.

ossie guffy

ALL MOTHERS ARE RICH WHEN THEY LOVE
THEIR CHILDREN.
THERE ARE NO POOR MOTHERS, NO UGLY ONES,
NO OLD ONES.
THEIR LOVE IS ALWAYS THE MOST BEAUTIFUL
OF THE JOYS.

maurice maeterlinck (1862 - 1949)

THE REAL SECRET BEHIND MOTHERHOOD… LOVE,
THE THING THAT MONEY CAN'T BUY.

anna crosby

...WHAT DO GIRLS DO WHO HAVEN'T ANY MOTHERS
TO HELP THEM THROUGH THEIR TROUBLES?

louisa may alcott (1832 - 1888)

WHO RAN TO HELP ME WHEN I FELL,

AND WHO WOULD SOME PRETTY STORY TELL,

OR KISS THE PLACE TO MAKE IT WELL?

MY MOTHER.

ann taylor

women
know

THE WAY TO REAR UP CHILDREN (TO BE JUST)

THEY KNOW A SIMPLE, MERRY, TENDER KNACK

OF TYING SASHES, FITTING BABY-SHOES,

AND STRINGING PRETTY WORDS

THAT MAKE NO SENSE,

AND KISSING FULL SENSE INTO EMPTY WORDS.

elizabeth barrett browning (1806 - 1861)

MOTHER LOVE IS THE FUEL THAT ENABLES A NORMAL
HUMAN BEING TO DO THE IMPOSSIBLE.

marion c. garretty, b.1917

ANYONE WHO THINKS MOTHER LOVE IS AS SOFT
AND GOLDEN-EYED AS A PURRING CAT SHOULD SEE
A CAT DEFENDING HER KITTENS.

pam brown, b.1928

SHE BROKE THE BREAD INTO TWO FRAGMENTS AND
GAVE THEM TO THE CHILDREN, WHO ATE WITH AVIDITY.
"SHE HATH KEPT NONE FOR HERSELF,"
GRUMBLED THE SERGEANT.
"BECAUSE SHE IS NOT HUNGRY," SAID A SOLDIER.
"BECAUSE SHE IS A MOTHER," SAID THE SERGEANT.

victor hugo (1802 - 1885)

MOTHERHOOD IS THE MOST EMOTIONAL
EXPERIENCE OF ONE'S LIFE. ONE JOINS A KIND
OF WOMAN'S MAFIA.

janet suzman

STRONG, BEAUTIFUL, HAPPY AND SUCCESSFUL
THOUGH HER OWN CHILDREN MAY BE, SOMEWHERE
IN THE INNER DARKNESS OF A WOMAN'S MIND LIE THE
RECOLLECTIONS OF THOSE OTHERS, THE CHILDREN,
BLOWN AWAY LIKE A FLURRY OF LEAVES BY SICKNESS,
SORROW AND DEVILRY, BY HUNGER AND BY WAR.
TO HAVE A CHILD IS TO GIVE HER A SHARE IN EVERY
CHILD AND SHE MOURNS THEM AS HER OWN.

pam brown, b.1928

NOW THAT I HAVE THESE CHILDREN,
I'M JUST CRAZED ABOUT THE WORLD'S MAKING IT
TO THE NEXT CENTURY.

meryl streep, b.1949

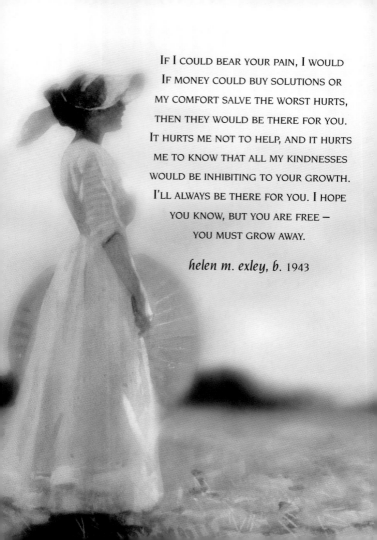

IF I COULD BEAR YOUR PAIN, I WOULD
IF MONEY COULD BUY SOLUTIONS OR
MY COMFORT SALVE THE WORST HURTS,
THEN THEY WOULD BE THERE FOR YOU.
IT HURTS ME NOT TO HELP, AND IT HURTS
ME TO KNOW THAT ALL MY KINDNESSES
WOULD BE INHIBITING TO YOUR GROWTH.
I'LL ALWAYS BE THERE FOR YOU. I HOPE
YOU KNOW, BUT YOU ARE FREE —
YOU MUST GROW AWAY.

helen m. exley, b. 1943

THE EVERLASTING SADNESS OF ANY
MOTHER IS THAT THERE COMES A TIME
WHEN SHE CAN NO LONGER BRING
MAGIC TO YOUR LIFE, NOR CURE
TO YOUR TROUBLES.

diana briscoe

THE OLDER I BECOME, THE MORE I THINK ABOUT MY MOTHER.

ingmar bergman (1915-1982)

IT DOESN'T MATTER HOW OLD I GET, WHENEVER I
SEE ANYTHING NEW OR SPLENDID, I WANT TO CALL,
"MOM, COME AND LOOK".

*helen m. exley, b.*1943

A MOTHER'S LOVE FOR THE CHILD OF HER BODY DIFFERS
ESSENTIALLY FROM ALL OTHER AFFECTIONS, AND BURNS WITH SO
STEADY AND CLEAR A FLAME THAT IT APPEARS LIKE THE ONE
UNCHANGEABLE THING IN THIS EARTHLY MUTABLE LIFE, SO THAT
WHEN SHE IS NO LONGER PRESENT IT IS STILL A LIGHT TO
OUR STEPS AND A CONSOLATION.

w. h. hudson (1841 - 1922)

MOTHER LOVE MAKES A WOMAN MORE
VULNERABLE THAN ANY OTHER CREATURE ON EARTH.

*pam brown, b.*1928

WHAT IS ASTONISHING, WHAT CAN GIVE US ENORMOUS HOPE AND BELIEF IN A FUTURE IN WHICH THE LIVES OF WOMEN AND CHILDREN SHALL BE AMENDED AND REWOVEN BY WOMEN'S HANDS, IS ALL THAT WE HAVE MANAGED TO SALVAGE, OF OURSELVES, FOR OUR CHILDREN [...] THE TENDERNESS, THE PASSION, THE TRUST IN OUR INSTINCTS, THE EVOCATION OF A COURAGE WE DID NOT KNOW WE OWNED, THE DETAILED APPREHENSION OF ANOTHER HUMAN EXISTENCE, THE FULL REALIZATION OF THE COST AND PRECARIOUSNESS OF LIFE. THE MOTHER'S BATTLE FOR HER CHILD — WITH SICKNESS, WITH POVERTY, WITH WAR, WITH ALL THE FORCES OF EXPLOITATION AND CALLOUSNESS THAT CHEAPEN HUMAN LIFE — NEEDS TO BECOME A COMMON HUMAN BATTLE, WAGED IN LOVE AND IN THE PASSION FOR SURVIVAL.

*adrienne rich, b.*1929

remembering...

THAT LOVELY VOICE; HOW I SHOULD WEEP FOR JOY
IF I COULD HEAR IT NOW!

colette (1873-1954)

YOU TOO, MY MOTHER, READ MY RHYMES
FOR LOVE OF UNFORGOTTEN TIMES,
AND YOU MAY CHANCE TO HEAR ONCE MORE
THE LITTLE FEET ALONG THE FLOOR.

robert louis stevenson (1850 - 1894)

THE ONLY GHOSTS, I BELIEVE, WHO CREEP INTO
THIS WORLD, ARE DEAD YOUNG MOTHERS, RETURNED
TO SEE HOW THEIR CHILDREN FARE. THERE IS NO
OTHER INDUCEMENT GREAT ENOUGH TO BRING THE
DEPARTED BACK.

j. m. barrie (1860 - 1937)

MY MOTHER WANTED ME TO BE HER WINGS, TO FLY
AS SHE NEVER QUITE HAD THE COURAGE TO DO.
I LOVE HER FOR THAT. I LOVE THE FACT THAT SHE
WANTED TO GIVE BIRTH TO HER OWN WINGS.

erica jong, b.1942

letting go

THE MOTHER-CHILD RELATIONSHIP IS PARADOXICAL
AND, IN A SENSE TRAGIC. IT REQUIRES THE MOST
INTENSE LOVE ON THE MOTHER'S SIDE, YET THIS VERY
LOVE MUST HELP THE CHILD GROW AWAY FROM THE
MOTHER AND BECOME FULLY INDEPENDENT.

erich fromm (1900 - 1980)

A MOTHER IS NOT A PERSON TO LEAN ON BUT A
PERSON TO MAKE LEANING UNNECCESSARY.

dorothy canfield fisher (1879 - 1958)

NOBODY CAN HAVE THE SOUL OF ME. MY MOTHER
HAS HAD IT, AND NOBODY CAN HAVE IT AGAIN.
NOBODY CAN COME INTO MY VERY SELF AGAIN, AND
BREATHE ME LIKE AN ATMOSPHERE.

d. h. lawrence (1885 - 1930)

THERE IS AN ENDURING TENDERNESS IN THE LOVE
OF A MOTHER.... IT IS NEITHER TO BE CHILLED BY
SELFISHNESS, NOR DAUNTED BY DANGER,.... SHE WILL
SACRIFICE EVERY COMFORT TO HIS CONVENIENCE;
SHE WILL SURRENDER EVERY PLEASURE TO HIS
ENJOYMENT; SHE WILL GLORY IN HIS FAME AND
EXALT IN HIS PROSPERITY; AND IF ADVERSITY
OVERTAKE HIM, HE WILL BE THE DEARER TO HER BY
MISFORTUNE; AND IF DISGRACE SETTLE UPON HIS
NAME, SHE WILL STILL LOVE AND CHERISH HIM; AND
IF ALL THE WORLD BESIDE CAST HIM OFF,
SHE WILL BE ALL THE WORLD TO HIM.

washington irving (1783 - 1859)

Dedication: To my lovely mother, you've given me everything you ever could. This collection says just some of the things I'd like to say in thanks. Helen.

Helen Exley Giftbooks cover the most powerful of all human relationships: love between couples, the bonds within families and between friends.

No expense is spared in making sure that each book is as thoughtful and meaningful a gift as it is possible to create: good to give, good to receive.

You have the result in your hands. If you have loved it — tell others! There is no power on earth like the word-of-mouth recommendation of friends.